DISCOVERING
YOUR PRESENCE

Claire Pickens

About the Author

Originally from the Wine Country of California, Claire has a range of experience that lends well to being an impactful speaker, author, entrepreneur, and coach. In her youth, her powerful 6-foot stature led to the evolution of a solid work ethic through her active participation in athletics. Claire was an avid equestrian, basketball player, and track and field athlete. Despite her drive and focus to succeed athletically, injuries prevented her ability to participate in college athletics. This drastic change in her path caused her to develop a humble nature that would ultimately make her a successful entrepreneur, speaker, and leader.

In 2003, she began on the design of her own brick-and-mortar business. By 2005, she successfully built and opened her business, bringing her athletic work ethic into the world of business to produce great results. Her humble, confident nature created a leadership presence that gained the trust of her staff. The combination of her experience and specialized knowledge earned her a Certified Veterinary Practice Manager (CVPM) certification.

Alongside business ownership, Claire has a plethora of athletic coaching experience. She has coached inside the public school system (basketball and track), as well as for recreational and player development programs. Her experience as a coach taught her a powerful leadership approach, which she then applied in the business world to increase employee performance. Coaching involves the continual use of concise communication skills. In this high-pressure environment, Claire saw that the strict disciplinary style of authority could remain positive and inspiring.

In 2016, Claire entered the realm of professional corporate speaking and training, logging over 250 hours in 50 venues on 14 topics throughout the year. She learned how to have a strong, engaging presence that keeps crowds interested for hours on end. Through talking with the audience, she learned that creating a strong presence is something people would like to achieve in business.

Her combination of experiences in and out of the business world have prepared her to be the ideal guide to developing a strong, impactful presence. She possesses a powerful yet humble nature that is empathetic to the difficulties of experiencing rapid change, understands the work ethic required to go through a growth process, and is ready to be your guide to achieving more targeted, powerful, and positive results from your professional interactions.

First Edition 2017

Printed by CreateSpace

ISBN   978-0-692-86169-1

DISCOVERING YOUR PRESENCE:
THE "HOW-TO" GUIDE TO USING THE WORKBOOK

The process of discovering and developing a strong presence requires introspection into how you see yourself and your perception of how others see you. How you see yourself is the most important factor in the development of a strong presence.

This workbook is meant as a guide and journal through your discovery process. Utilize the blank note pages to journal additional thoughts, set goals, or document moments in your life that come to mind as we tackle the different components of the discovery process.

No doubt there were times in your life where your presence was very strong. Times where your confidence soared, and you could walk into situations *standing tall*. This may have been in personal or professional situations, but both are equally important to journal as you go through this workbook. Through this discovery process, the goal is to tap into your strengths. Rather than focusing on negativity, I'd like you to focus on how you will use strengths you already possess to create a strong presence. Through the journaling of past experiences, you'll be able to make a note of scenarios and situations where your presence came naturally. We will begin to differentiate your personal presence from your professional presence. We will tap into your natural ability to create a strong presence and utilize that in your professional interactions to achieve more targeted professional results.

Be honest and genuine as you continue through this discovery process. This workbook is the foundation to *Stepping Up Your Presence*. While you may find yourself seeking input from others regarding the content in this workbook, I encourage you to keep this discovery process a private one so that you can be 100% transparent.

Time to STAND TALL and begin DISCOVERING YOUR PRESENCE!

I'm honored to be a part of your discovery process,

Claire Pickens

Creator of the STAND TALL concept of Maximizing Presence to Boost Performance

CONTENTS

DEFINING PRESENCE

The development of a strong presence begins with defining what the word *presence* means to you. As you go through the process of discovering how you will grow and strengthen your presence, refer back to this page. It will serve as a point of reference to the growth process. During this process, it is possible that *presence* takes on a new meaning for you. Before you give *presence* your own definition, I'd like you to ask yourself a few questions.

> *"I stopped trying to be perfect when I realized it's enough to be present."*
>
> - Curtis Tyrone Jones

Does the definition of presence differ between personal and professional interactions?

....

....

Does presence have anything to do with your impact on others?

....

....

Does presence involve any of your physical characteristics?

....

....

Throughout the workbook, you will notice that you have ample space to make additional notes. This is a great way to reflect on times in your life where a different type of presence would have had an impact as well as an opportunity to give yourself credit when your presence was just as it needed to be.

MAXIMIZE THE POWER OF THIS WORKBOOK BY:

1) acknowledging attributes that require adjustment or change

2) acknowledging attributes you are currently happy with

3) reflecting on moments past, present, and future that will benefit from you becoming more aware of your presence

HOW OTHERS DEFINE PRESENCE:
PERSONAL

Presence is a word that is often defined differently by people with different cultures, backgrounds, upbringings, and beliefs. Upon speaking with people about defining a personal presence, I gathered some intriguing definitions from all over the world. Are there any definitions that resonate with you? Utilize the journaling space to make note of the vocabulary and phrasing that catches your attention.

> *"A powerful presence begins with creating an intent for the impact you'd like to have in your interactions with others."*
>
> *-Claire Pickens*

How do you define your personal presence?

....

....

Male responses:

- Being in the moment with others.
- Being with someone and with your full attention and love.
- Real and in the moment.
- What's left when ego is released.
- Heightened sense of conscious awareness; an alignment of your consciousness with your source.
- The manner in which a person carries themselves. The self-confidence a person has in themselves and in the way they can captivate their audience, whether that is one person or a thousand.
- To be a participant in your life and of others, and not just exist in it.
- The gift of consciously recognizing and appreciating all that life was, is, and shall become.

Female responses:

- Awareness of one's own self, and an awareness by others towards you.
- Being where your hands and feet are!
- Someone who is emotionally strong-minded can have a presence when they walk into a room. It's like you know they are there.
- Spirit.
- Paying attention to the people you are with.
- When someone has presence, it means stay power or to remember.
- Firstly, being fully in the moment (not thinking of the past or future). Secondly, it's an energy, a flow, being in your heat and radiating that out. Like when performers have "***presence.***"
- Sweet personality.

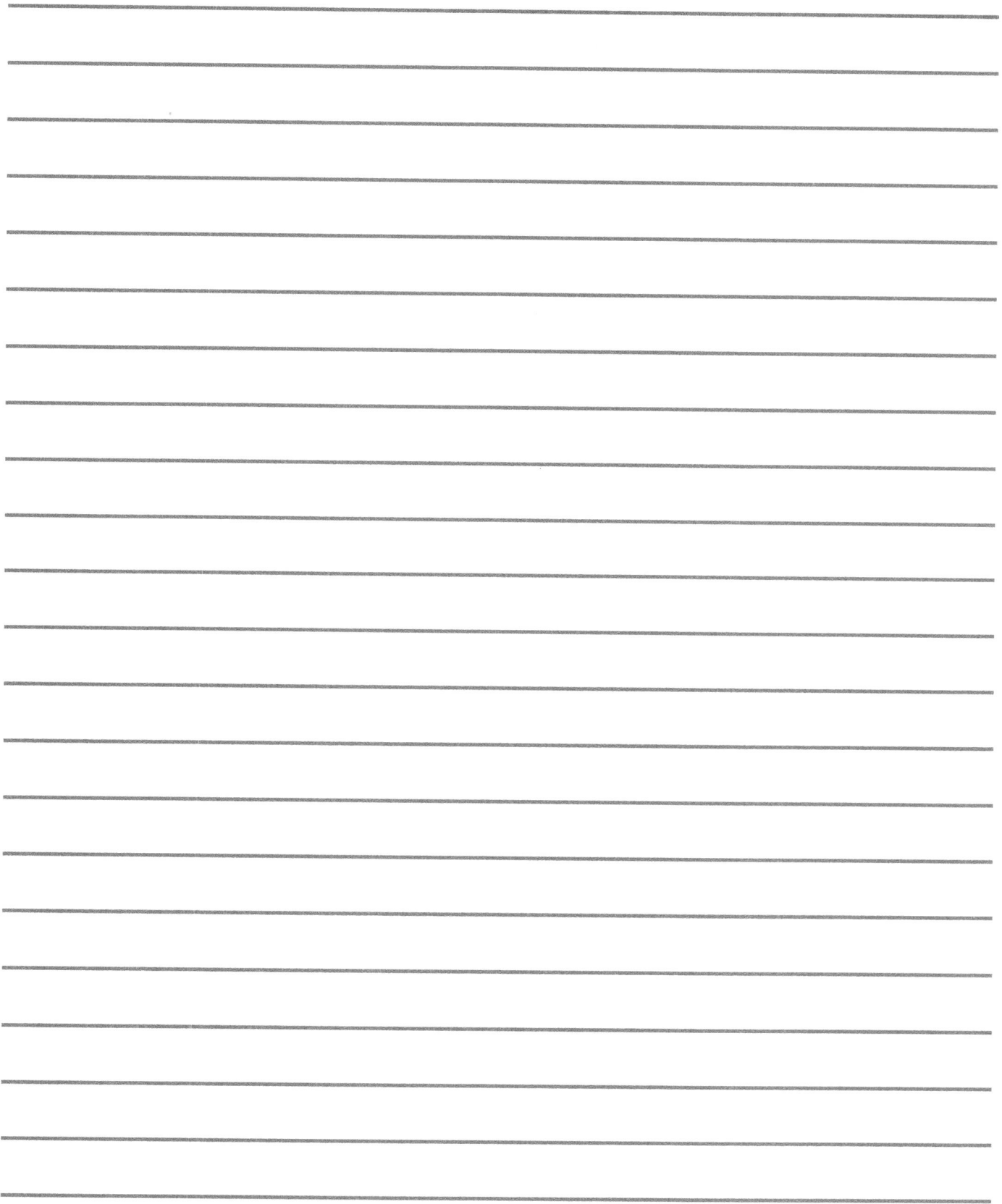

HOW OTHERS DEFINE PRESENCE:
PROFESSIONAL

"An entrepreneur's presence strengthens with the ability to simultaneously maintain a strong vision for the future, and stay grounded in the day-to-day operation of the business."

-Claire Pickens

The same question was asked from a professional standpoint, and resulted in some slightly different answers. Are there any of these professional presence definitions that resonate with you? Make note of any key words or phrases that catch your attention. It is time to think about differentiating your personal presence from your professional presence. Think specifically about your professional presence and how you want to impact your interactions.

How do you define professional presence?

....

....

Male Responses:

- Ask questions, listen, comment briefly, and then ask questions.
- Engaging and attentive.
- Bringing a purpose with excellent listening and interaction skills! Being prepared and focused!
- Combination of active listening, strength-based feedback, and a clear sense of purpose.
- Just "being." Focused on the person or group. Your personal energy or aura. It makes me want to meet you.
- It depends on the specific social dynamic. A sales rep will take a different attack than a strategic advisor. It relates to the hierarchy of power and the desired outcome.
- It means others immediately expect good input from you.
- To actively perform your duty on certain tasks to come up with an excellent result.
- Bring passion and honesty!
- Confidence.
- On time! With Mr. Smell's good plumber attitude. {reference to local commercial}

Female responses:

- Polished. Smart. Sharp. Knowledgeable.
- Confidence and to pay attention to people! Just a bit of eye contact and a handshake before a meeting makes all the difference as to how you are received by others.
- Look and act sharp!
- Looking, acting, and performing in the way you would be expected to in an environment. Being the person you need to be in whatever situation. Professional is one kind of presence, but there are other uniforms that we are assigned to wear in life.

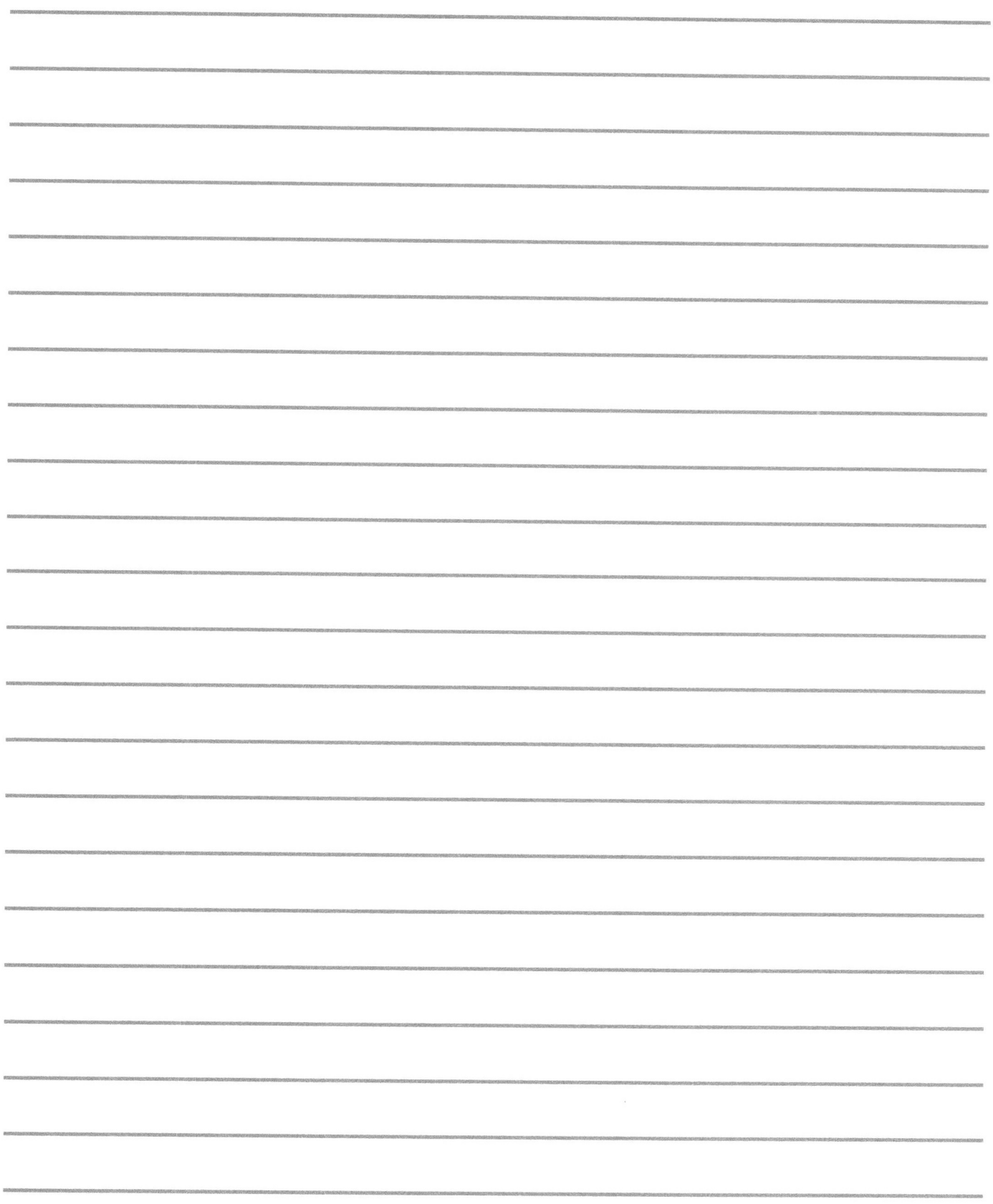

IDENTIFYING YOUR STRONGEST
PERSONAL & PROFESSIONAL
TRAITS

What is your perception of your strongest professional traits? Think about the physical, intellectual, professional, and moral attributes that have a positive impact on your presence. Look at all the following words and circle any that you feel are descriptive of your strongest traits. Utilize the journaling page to note specific times that any of the traits you identified have had a strong positive impact on your professional performance or personal relationships.

Accountable	Flexible
Assertive	Focused
Adventurous	Honest
Approachable	Independent
Articulate	Insightful
Autonomous	Meticulous
Calm	Organized
Charismatic	Patient
Cheerful	Persistent
Clever	Persuasive
Confident	Physically Attractive
Concise Communicator	Physically Strong
Cooperative	Punctual
Devoted	Resourceful
Efficient	Responsible
Eloquent	Speak with Clarity
Empathetic	Technological
Energetic	
Enthusiastic	

YOUR STRONGEST TRAITS: PROFESSIONAL

To be able to create and maintain a strong professional presence, you must identify your strongest traits. From the traits you have already identified, choose the 5 strongest traits that contribute to your professional presence. These traits are those that allow you to have an intentional impact in your professional interactions.

1...

2...

3...

4...

5...

How will you accentuate these traits in your professional conduct?

....

How will you translate these traits into success?

....

Are these traits a part of your resume?

....

Utilize the journaling page to create an introduction ("elevator speech") in which you use your most powerful traits to describe who you are.

Example: Organized, Assertive, Leader, Concise Communication, Approachable

I am an approachable leader that has the ability to communicate concisely to a team and implement assertive action from all members to reach goals in an organized fashion.

YOUR STRONGEST TRAITS:
PERSONAL

The creation of a strong professional presence involves understanding how your personal and professional traits intertwine. From the traits chosen on Page 12, choose the 5 that best represent your personal presence. Choose the traits that contribute most to the maintenance of healthy personal relationships. Choose the traits that you feel makes you a good friend, partner, spouse, parent, or member of the community.

1 ....

2 ....

3 ....

4 ....

5 ....

How are these traits maintaining strong personal relationships?

....

How will you use them to keep your personal relationships moving in a positive direction?

....

Do any of these traits also apply to your professional presence?

....

....

Are your professional and personal strengths helping or hurting each other?

....

....

Utilize the journaling page to identify moments where these traits have had a positive contribution to your personal relationships and interactions.

YOUR WEAKEST ATTRIBUTES

The identification of weakness is an important step to building a presence that maintains a consistency of strength. Genuinely accepting and identifying traits inhibiting your communication and relationships with others will allow you to set tangible goals for growth. Circle any of the traits below that apply to you, as well as add any that are not listed.

Addictive Personality

Aggressive

Blames Others

Bossy

Close-minded

Commanding

Conservative

Dismissive

Disorganized

Don't like Physical Appearance

Fear of Change

Forgetful

Gossip

Have The Last Word

Impatient

Impulsive

....

....

Inconsistent

Indecisive

Inflated Ego

Judgmental

Lack Confidence

Lack Empathy

Lack transparency

Not Punctual

Opinionated

Passive

Poor Communicator

Poor Listening Skills

Resistant to Training

Slow to Change

Work-a-holic

....

....

....

How are these traits inhibiting your ability to have productive relationships and interactions with other people?

....

....

How long have you been aware of your weakest traits?

....

Which 3 traits are you going to set a goal to immediately improve upon?

....

LOSS OF PRESENCE:
PERSONAL

There are events in our lives that impact the way we interact with others. These events impact our internal dialogue and significantly impact our confidence levels. Sometimes this affects only our personal interactions, but often it spills into our professional interactions. Take a moment to think about the events in your life that have impacted your confidence, way of thinking, and way of interacting with others. Think about those times that may have caused you to lose your personal presence.

Accident

Accumulation of Debt

Break Up

Change in Appearance: Dental

Change in Appearance: Other

Change in Appearance: Scars

Change in Appearance: Weight

Child Leaving Home

....

....

....

Custody Issues

Death

Divorce

Foreclosure/Eviction

Injury

Medical Diagnosis

Relocation

....

....

....

....

How did these events impact your interactions with other people?

....

....

Are these events still impacting your personal and professional interactions?

....

Have you set a goal to reduce the negative impact they are having on your personal and professional presence?

....

LOSS OF PRESENCE:
PROFESSIONAL

There are events that occur in our professional lives that impact our professional confidence. These events cause either a positional shift, income shift, or attitude shift. When we experience these shifts, it often impacts the way we interact with others in our professional environments. The impact can be as large as the loss of confidence, enthusiasm, purpose, or hope of positive results, or the change happens gradually over time, causing a complacency that results in less impactful interactions with others professionally. Take a moment to reflect on your career and identify any moments that had a negative impact on your professional presence.

Benefit loss

Bored in position

Burnt out in industry

Change of industry

Demotion

Discrimination (age, sex, race, religion, culture)

Failed early retirement

Failed entrepreneurial venture

Failed project

Failed promotion (got position but did not transition well)

Failed to reach company objectives/goals as a leader

Failed to reach company objectives/goals as an individual

Feeling underemployed

Income reduction

Lack of certification(s)

Lack of funds to pursue continuing education

Lack of graduate degree

Lack of high school diploma

Lack of skills to stay competitive

Lack of undergraduate degree

Layoff

Leave of absence impacted position

Office politics

Overqualified for position

Passed up for promotion

Promotion not available

Reduction from full time to part time

Relocation

Right degree but cannot find job to fit needs/personality

Termination

Transfer

Wrong degree and not interested in degree field

....

....

....

....

POINT OF INTERSECTION:
WHERE PERSONAL & PROFESSIONAL LOSS INTERSECT

Top 3 professional events you allowed to impact your personal presence

1. ....

2. ....

3. ....

Top 3 personal events you allowed to impact your professional presence

1. ....

2. ....

3. ....

Events that crossed over and impacted both realms negatively

....

....

What events will you no longer allow to cross from one realm to the next?

....

....

Has your professional performance been impacted by personal events?

....

....

Have your personal relationships been impacted by professional events?

....

....

Moving forward, can you see how a separation of personal and professional presence will allow you to maintain healthy relationships and high professional performance? While it is inevitable that drastic events will impact multiple realms of our lives, it is also essential that we establish healthy boundaries so that successes can still occur amidst difficult situations. Use this point of intersection to reflect on the areas of your life that can improve with the establishment of health, personal, and professional boundaries with your presence. Utilize the journaling page to elaborate on the questions in this page.

POINT OF INTERSECTION:
YOUR STRONGEST TRAITS

Earlier, you identified your strongest personal and professional traits and separated them into two different lists. Take a moment now and re-combine those lists into your 5 strongest overall traits—traits that will keep your performance high and relationships healthy in both your personal and professional realms. These are the traits you will carry from your personal to professional presence to create a seamless and genuine transition.

1 ....

2 ....

3 ....

4 ....

5 ....

Are you currently conveying these traits in the way you interact with others personally and professionally?

....

....

How will these traits improve communication personally and professionally?

....

....

....

....

The 5 traits you identified here are what you view as your strongest traits. They are essential to the discovery and development of a strong, impactful presence. To perform professionally, you will need to bring these traits into your daily interactions. Personally, these traits will reveal your confidence to others and create healthy relationships based upon your best qualities. Keep this list of traits in a place that is regularly visible. Remind yourself what makes you genuinely strong, and exhibit these traits in your interactions with others.

LABELS THAT
PARALYZE PRESENCE

Negative labels are counterproductive to positive thinking. Anything counterproductive to thinking positively about yourself will impact your ability to maintain a strong presence. These labels create a self-dialogue that often plays in our heads before we enter personal and professional situations. Commonly, the labels originate in one realm and cross over to the other realm, creating a negative impact on confidence. Look at these labels and identify if any of them have been assigned to you, self-assigned, or have impacted your presence personally or professionally at any point in your life.

Angry	Freak	Not Good Enough	Short
Big	Hopeless	OCD/ Perfectionist	Shy
Boring	Hyper	Old	Sloppy
Bully	Lanky	Pathetic	Slow
Crazy	Lazy	Pig	Stupid
Different	Liar	Psycho	Ugly
Dumb	Loser	Pushover	Unapproachable
Emotional	Lousy	Quitter	Unattractive
Failure	Mean	Racial Slur	Underachiever
Fat	Negative	Self-centered	Weird
Flat	Nerd		Worthless

Utilize the journaling space to identify when, where, and under what circumstances these labels became a part of your life.

When entering a situation, the conversation you have with yourself prior to entry is vitally important to your presence. If you are applying negative self-labels to yourself before you enter the room, your presence will be negatively impacted.

Which of these labels do you think is having the biggest negative impact on your professional presence?

....

....

Are you ready to start removing these negative labels so that you can maximize your professional performance?

....

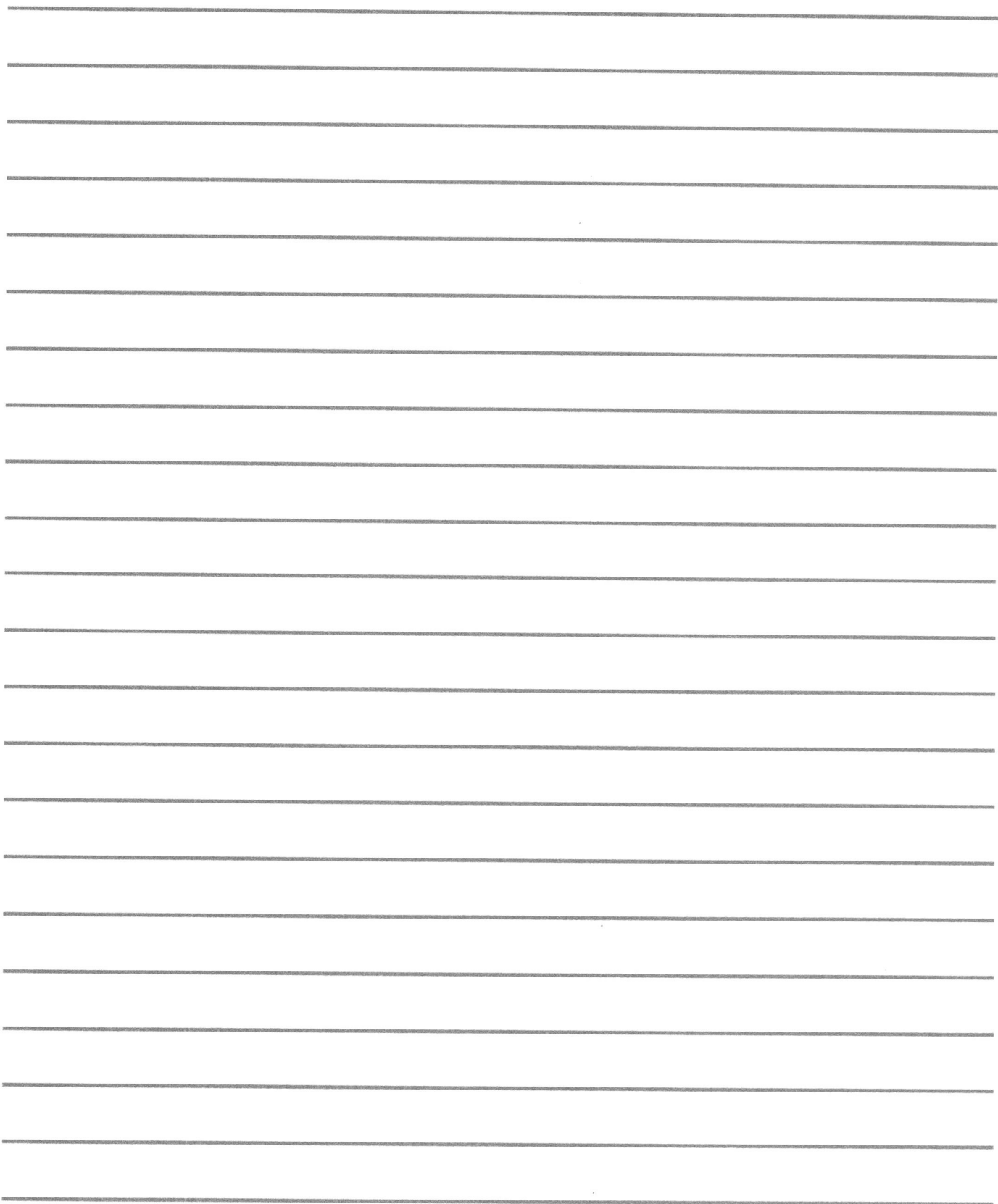

LABELS THAT
MAXIMIZE PRESENCE

To create the right kind of self-dialogue, speak to yourself in terms of your strongest traits and most positive labels. Identify the positive labels you have assigned to yourself, or others have assigned to you, that boost your confidence. Regular use of these positive labels in your own self-dialogue will contribute to a more confident presence personally and professionally. Utilize the journaling space to explain how these labels positively impact your confidence.

Artistic	Humble
Athletic	Impactful
Attractive	Innovative
Beautiful	Inspiring
Charming	Intelligent
Collaborative	Intuitive
Compassionate	Perceptive
Competitive	Popular
Creative	Powerful
Dependable	Professional
Disciplined	Selective
Encouraging	Selfless
Engaged	Sexy
Faithful	Sincere
Funny	Spiritual
Generous	Strong
Gentle	Understanding
Gifted	Valuable
Handsome	Vibrant
Happy	....
....	....
....	....

THE IMPACT OF
NEGATIVE SELF-DIALOGUE ON PROFESSIONAL PRESENCE

Negative self-dialogue produces negative results. It does not set the

stage for success and often leads to further negative self-dialogue. What you convince yourself as true about yourself becomes the image you bring of yourself into your interactions.

From the list of negative labels, choose 5 that you are allowing to impact your professional presence.

1
....

2
....

3
....

4
....

5
....

Identify the label that you will eliminate first from your professional self-dialogue. Why is this label having the biggest impact on your professional interactions?

....

....

....

Of these labels, which were assigned in your personal life and carried over to your professional life?

....

....

Which of these labels originally assigned in the professional realm are you allowing to impact your personal relationships?

....

....

As you move forward in discovering and developing a powerful presence, make it a priority to remove these negative labels from your self-dialogue. Understand that you cannot have the powerful impact you'd like to have if you are thinking negatively about your character, skills, personality, or physical appearance.

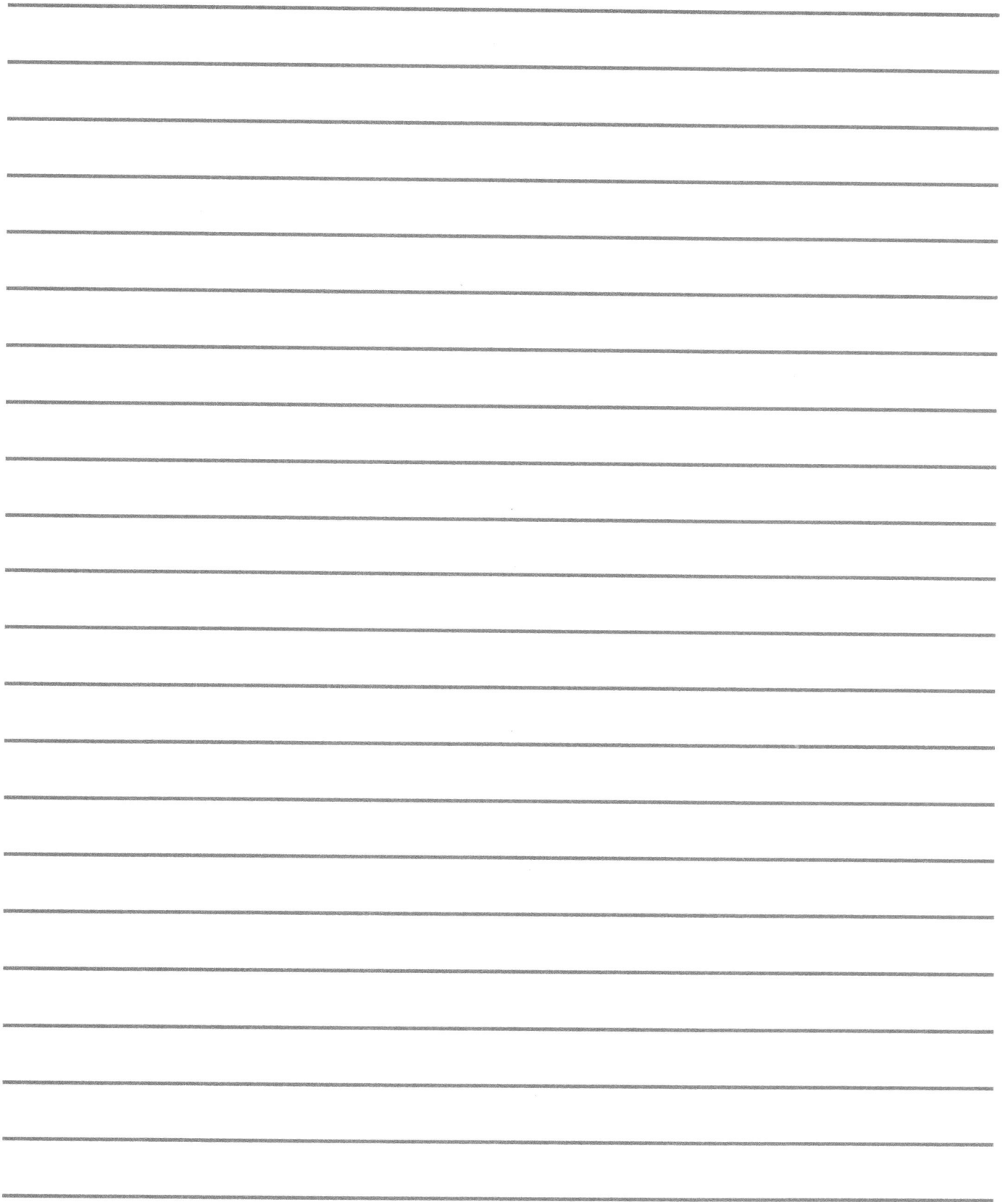

SEEING THE BEST IN YOURSELF:
POSITIVE PROFESSIONAL LABELS

From the list of positive labels, identify the 5 you feel are your strongest labels applicable to your professional presence. Going forward, you will use these labels to create a positive self-dialogue before your interactions. They will contribute in creating an image of yourself that is built for success. Using positive self-dialogue allows you to become more targeted in the goals you set for the results you'd like to achieve in your professional interactions.

Utilize the journaling page to reflect on moments where positive self-dialogue would have had, or will have, a powerful impact on your ability in having a strong presence in your professional interactions.

1 ....

2 ....

3 ....

4 ....

5 ....

Don't wait for others to give you a compliment to boost your confidence. You are already aware of your strongest traits and can give yourself compliments. Recognize the best in yourself: Use those traits and labels to achieve your goals.

Of these top 5 labels, which will become the biggest asset in your professional interactions?

....

....

How can these labels help you maintain and build healthy, long-term professional relationships?

....

....

How will these labels help you achieve your goals?

....

....

POINT OF INTERSECTION:
RELABELING YOURSELF FOR PROFESSIONAL SUCCESS

List your top 5 positive and negative self-labels next to each other. The contradiction between your self-perceived strongest and weakest traits often causes confusion regarding your ability to have a powerful presence. Being humble enough to appreciate your weaknesses, and confident enough to embrace your strengths, will allow you to build and maintain a strong presence that comes across as genuine, strong, and purposeful.

Top 5 Positive Labels	Top 5 Negative Labels
1	1 ....
2	2 ....
3	3 ....
4	4 ....
5	5 ....

In your self-dialogue, are you balanced?

....

Do you speak to yourself in terms of your positive labels as much or more than you speak to yourself about your negative labels?

....

When you are in professional situations, do you allow the negative labels to drive your dialogue and demeanor?

....

When a label is assigned, do you internalize and alter your actions and reactions based on that label? (Example: being called aggressive while exhibiting assertive traits, or being called passive when you are attempting to be a good listener)

....

Are you allowing the labels others assign to you to drive your professional confidence and presence?

....

Utilize the journal page to elaborate on your ability to balance your acknowledgment of both your positive and negative traits and labels. Write about occurrences in your personal and professional life where you allowed another person's opinion impact your presence.

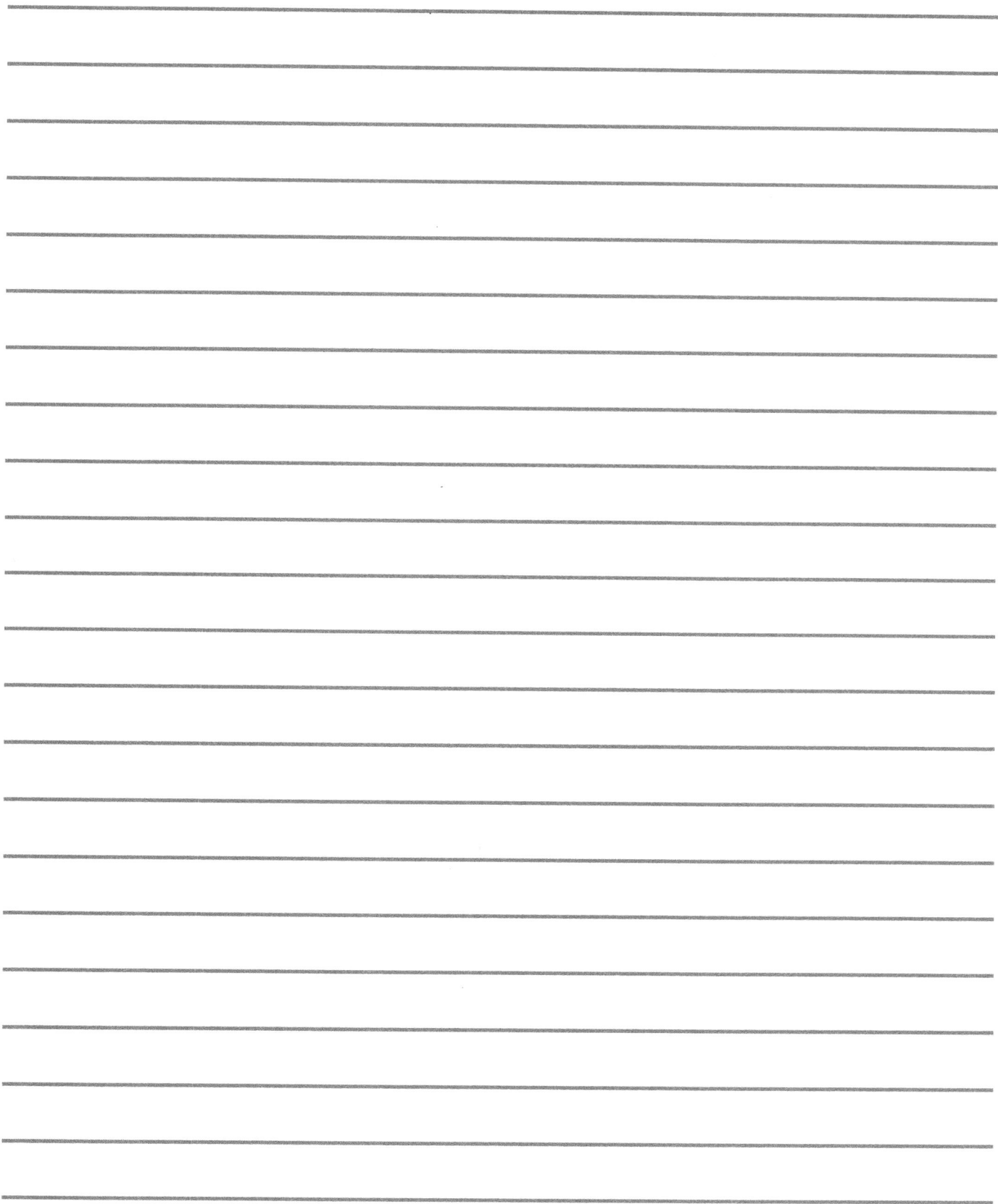

PUTTING IT ALL TOGETHER:
SEPARATING YOUR PERSONAL & PROFESSIONAL PRESENCE

It can be extremely detrimental to allow the stresses or negativity from either the personal or professional realm to cross over and impact the other. As we have gone through the discovery process, we have made a clear effort to draw a distinction between your personal and professional life. Creating healthy boundaries will allow you to experience success in both realms, regardless of the failures that may occur in either. To maintain a strong presence in both realms, you must remain aware of your strengths in each.

As we have gone through the discovery process, have you discovered a crossover between your personal and professional presence?

....

....

Have you allowed your personal self-dialogue and self-labelling to inappropriately interfere with your professional interactions?

....

....

Are there healthy boundaries that you will establish, because of this discovery process, to maximize your professional presence?

....

....

Are there healthy boundaries that you will establish, because of this discovery process, to improve your personal relationships?

....

....

PUTTING IT ALL TOGETHER:
YOUR UNIQUELY STRONG PRESENCE

"Acknowledge and rejuvenate your most powerful traits to maintain and build a strong presence."

-Claire Pickens

The discovery process included the acknowledgment of triumphs and losses. It personally and professionally required the acknowledgment of your strongest traits , and it revealed the labels that are helping and hurting you the most.

It's time to put it all together to decide the type of impact you'd like to have in both your personal and professional interactions. It is time to define what a strong presence means to you.

How will you define your professional presence from this point forward?

....

....

....

How will you define your personal presence from this point forward?

....

....

....

How will you make your presence more POWERFUL and IMPACTFUL in professional situations?

....

....

....

Which strengths will you draw on specifically to ensure that you get the results you want and need?

....

....

PUTTING IT ALL TOGETHER:
GOAL SETTING

Does a stronger presence have the potential to help you

"Potential is only as good as the actions implemented to utilize the talents you possess."

-Claire Pickens

ach eve your goals? Potential is only realized when tangible goa s are set. Goals that are intelligently designed to utilize the strengths we have been discovering throughout this workbook. Goals that realistically align with your talents, abilities, and time management skills.

To set intelligent goals, let us first break them into six categories. Within each category, write down at least 3 goals.

1)   A goal you are willing to begin working on immediately

2)   A goal you will aim to achieve within 1 year

3)   A goal you will aim to achieve within 5 years

Personal Relationships

1.

2.

3.

Academic/Certifications

1.

2.

3.

Lifestyle/Vacation/Possessions

1.

2.

3.

Personal Relationships

1.

2.

3.

Promotions/Career

1.

2.

3.

Family/Children/Parents

1.

2.

3.

Utilize the journaling page to expand upon any of these goals to provide more specificity to what you would like to accomplish. Include a more specific timeline, resources required, or any other vital information essential to accomplishing that goal.

PUTTING IT ALL TOGETHER:
CONCLUSION

Thank you for your commitment to this discovery process. I hope, as you have gone through each page, that you have genuinely answered each question towards the pursuit of building a strong presence. The intent of this discovery process was not to change who you are; the intent was to connect you with your strongest traits so that you can present the strongest version of yourself in situations that will contribute to your overall success.

To best utilize the content YOU have written in this workbook:

1) Practice positive self-dialogue daily.
2) Practice removing negative self-dialogue daily.
3) Commit to setting healthy boundaries between your personal and professional realms.
4) Decide which personal and professional events you will continue to allow to impact your presence in each realm.
5) Develop short phrases, using the traits and labels we identified in this workbook, you will repeat to yourself daily to reaffirm your strengths.
6) Identify the traits that will be utilized to achieve your goals.

STAND TALL and recognize that you currently possess strengths and traits that will contribute in achieving a strong presence that conveys confidence and has a lasting impact. A strengths-based approach that allows you to set goals to achieve more targeted results in your interactions, both personally and professionally.

You've just begun the process of building a strong presence. Review this workbook often to check your progress. Utilize the journaling pages at the end of this workbook to document the growth process. Make note of how your new self-dialogue is impacting your ability to interact with others. Be genuine about the struggle to eliminate negative self-dialogue. Make note of your discipline in acting to achieve the goals you have written throughout this workbook.

STEPPING UP YOUR PRESENCE (the next workbook in this series) is an essential part of personal and professional growth. The consistent achievement of goals works hand in hand with how you present yourself in different situations. Understanding WHO you want to be. Recognizing WHAT type of impact you would like to have. Knowing WHEN a strong presence will have the most impact. Understanding WHERE to use your different types of presence to create a positive last impression. And most importantly, WHY having a strong presence will be beneficial to your life, both personally and professionally.

I look forward to continuing this process with you throughout my workbook series.

Claire Pickens

Creator of the STAND TALL concept of Maximizing Presence to Boost Performance

www.ingramcontent.com/pod-product-compliance
Lightning Source LLC
Chambersburg PA
CBHW081152040426
42445CB00015B/1857